MASK MAGIC

MASK
MAGIC

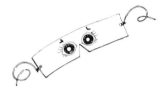

by
Carolyn Meyer

Illustrated by Melanie Gaines Arwin

Harcourt Brace Jovanovich
New York and London

Printed in the United States of America

First edition
B C D E F G H I J K

Library of Congress Cataloging in Publication Data

Meyer, Carolyn.
Mask magic.

Includes index.
SUMMARY: Information on how masks have been used by
various peoples over the centuries and directions for
making similar masks out of easily available materials.
1. Masks—Juvenile literature.   [1. Masks.
2. Handicraft]   I. Arwin, Melanie Gaines.   II. Title.
TT898.M48   731′.75   77–14080
ISBN 0–15–253107–6

Contents

CHAPTER 1

Mask Makers
and Mask Wearers

People have been making and wearing masks since the earliest days of mankind, when they first discovered that concealed behind a different face they could become somebody—or something—else. Masks seem to have a magical quality connected with them.

Nearly every culture in the world has made and

worn masks for some reason. On the walls of a cave in southwestern France, there are paintings of Stone Age men wearing the heads of animals. North American Indians draped themselves in animal skins, with the head attached, so they could sneak up on their prey unobserved. In Africa, masks were made to represent the spirits of dead ancestors. In the South Pacific, it was thought that masks offered protection from supernatural spirits.

The earliest masks were worn by primitive people in their religious rites, and their ritual dances made the lifeless masks seem animated. As religious ceremonies gradually changed into drama, both mask and movement continued to be important. When words spoken by the mask wearers also became important, the construction of the masks had to be changed.

In ancient Greece, dramas were performed in huge outdoor amphitheaters. It was difficult for the audience to see and hear what was happening on the stage, so the actors wore large masks that could clearly be seen at a distance, with special speaking tubes built into them that projected the voice. Since only three actors were permitted to perform in one play, masks allowed each actor to play several parts, including female roles.

Centuries later, priests of the Roman Catholic Church wore masks to enact religious dramas. These miracle plays and mystery plays, based on Bible stories and the lives of saints, were later taken out of the churches and performed in courtyards and marketplaces.

In the fourteenth century, the *commedia dell'arte,* "comedy of art," developed in Italy. The same characters appeared over and over in a few basic plots, and the actors improvised the dialogue as they went along. They wore half-masks, called *dominos,* which covered only the upper part of the face and helped to identify the characters. The audiences became familiar with both the characters and the plots and loudly cheered their favorites.

Unlike *commedia dell'arte,* which varied with

each performance, the *Noh* plays of Japan—also developed in the fourteenth century—were highly stylized, each movement and each speech done precisely as it had been done before. Originally there may have been thousands of these very short, slow-moving, and often puzzling plays; today about 250 of them still exist. Men play all the roles, using at least 125 kinds of full-face masks made of lacquered wood.

At the beginning of the seventeenth century in England, playwright Ben Jonson introduced the *masque,* an elaborate production in which professional actors and crowds of amateurs took part in the entertainment that included acting, dancing, singing, and miming. The performers wore fanciful costumes, and they wore masks.

In the same century a form of drama called the mumming play was developed around the legend of St. George and the dragon. Mummers, as the masked and costumed actors were called, put on these plays around Christmastime. But the presence of so many people in masks resulted in an increase in crime around the Christmas holidays, and the plays were eventually forbidden. They have been revived in a few English villages today.

At about this time, women started appearing on the stage, wearing a version of the domino, a small velvet eye mask called a *loup*. It was so flattering that many other women adopted this stage mask as part of their makeup, to conceal a bad complexion as well as to lend an air of mystery to their appearance.

Mask making is an ancient and prestigious craft. Traditional masks were often intricately constructed and required considerable skill. Many were so beautifully designed and executed that they were considered works of art. Even today, collectors prize the carved ivory masks of Africa, the jewel-encrusted masks of the ancient Aztecs, and the exquisitely lacquered Japanese *Noh* masks, as well as the sophisticated work of contemporary artists who make abstract and impressionistic masks from metal, fabric, and other materials.

Mask Makers and Mask Wearers

Masks have been made from an enormous variety of materials, including feathers and stone, but all of the masks in this book are created from inexpensive, easily available materials with the use of simple techniques. You can make masks that are beautiful, funny, or horrible; primitive or contemporary; realistic or like nothing that ever existed before. By following the step-by-step directions, you can easily reproduce the masks described. Or you can use these basic techniques as starting points to design your own creations. You can concentrate on making a simple mask with bold designs for quick effect, or you can invest a great deal of time and effort on your mask, working every detail to perfection, so that it becomes a collector's item.

The four seasons of the year have always been important in both primitive cultures and civilized societies. Many of the holidays we observe today are, in fact, based on ancient beliefs about the changing seasons. This book suggests designs for theatrical masks for summer, spirit masks for fall and Halloween, carnival masks for winter holidays, and realistic portrait masks for driving out the witches and demons of spring.

There is magic in masks—first when you transform ordinary materials into something extraordinary, and again when you put on the finished mask and for a little while take on a new identity. Without necessarily believing in the primitive magic of the early mask wearers, you can create some mask magic of your own.

CHAPTER 2

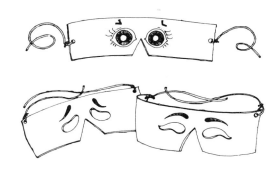

Theatrical Masks of Summer:
Half Masks

Let's start with summer. Midsummer Night was the ancient celebration of the summer solstice, the shortest night and the longest day of the year. On that night supernatural beings supposedly cavorted, human beings frolicked around huge bonfires, and young lovers found each other. It's a joyous festival that has inspired many artists, writers, and musicians: Shakespeare wrote the play *A Midsummer Night's Dream,* and the twentieth-century British composer Benjamin Britten wrote an opera by that name. Felix Mendelssohn's Overture to *A Midsummer Night's Dream* has become the traditional wedding music to which countless brides have walked down the aisle.

You can celebrate the joys of summer with masks —and perhaps *masques*—of your own making, disguising yourself and your friends as supernatural beings, lovers, clowns, animals, or whatever you wish. Paper heavy enough to hold its shape, but light enough to cut and bend easily, is ideal for the masks because it is a good background for painting or drawing features, and it is comfortable to wear.

Paper Half Masks

The basic half mask is simple to make. The challenge is in decorating it—by painting and drawing, by adding other features (horns, ears, whiskers), by embellishing it with yarn, fur, or feathers, or by enhancing it with hats and headdresses.

Theatrical Masks of Summer: Half Masks

Some half masks were quite elaborate. They covered not only the eyes but sometimes also the nose and the forehead, extending into elaborate headdresses. Paper can be used for both simple and elaborate half masks.

What you will need:

For the basic mask: Scrap paper; stiff paper or lightweight cardboard that bends without cracking, such as thin poster board, construction paper, drawing paper, a file folder, a paper plate, or a manila envelope; pencil, ruler, and scissors; string; crayons or tempera (poster) paints and paintbrushes.

For elaborate masks: Glue, tape, and staples; yarn, thick string, or paper strips for hair and whiskers; beads, feathers, fake fur, leather, large sequins, etc.

How to construct the basic mask:

1. *To make the pattern:* Cut a strip of paper 3½ inches by 11 inches. Fold the strip in half lengthwise and again crosswise. Open it out flat and make a mark where the folds intersect. Fold again crosswise. Measure ¾ inch from the fold along the bot-

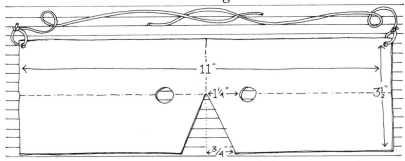

tom edge. Make a mark and cut from there through the folded paper to the center mark. That makes room for your nose. To locate the eyes, measure 1¼ inches from the center mark along the lengthwise fold. Cut out ½-inch circles, one on each side of the center mark. Try on the pattern to find out if you can see well. If you cannot, take off the pattern, make the circles larger or move them nearer or farther from the center mark. *Never* cut the pattern when you are wearing it.

2. Use the pattern for drawing a half mask on stiff paper or lightweight cardboard. Cut out the mask. Punch a hole near each end (the mask fits best if the hole is placed in the middle) and tie a piece of string about 12 inches long through each hole.

How to paint the eyes:

Since the eyes are the most important feature of the face, you'll want to paint or draw extraordinary eyes to convey the character you have in mind.

The shape of the eye, the way it slants, and the angle of the eyebrows all combine to make a face appear happy, sad, scared, angry, and so on. Study pictures of faces, the faces of people around you, and especially your own face in the mirror to find out what makes an "expression." On a piece of plain paper, draw two dots 2½ inches apart for the pupils of the eyes. Then draw simple sketches around them, using only a few bold lines to exaggerate the expression.

When you are experimenting, you'll find crayons easier to use because they are flexible enough to let you make slight changes, emphasizing a line here and an angle there. Poster paints give sharper lines and clearer colors, but they are more difficult to control. Here are a few ideas to help you experiment:

Tragedy and comedy: These are the traditional

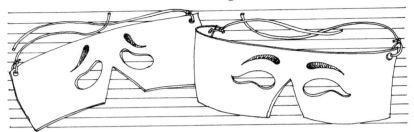

masks of the classical Greek theater. In the tragic mask, the eyebrows and eyes slant down at the outside corners. In the comic mask, the eyes slant up at the corners, as though crinkled up by a laugh, and the eyebrows are slightly raised. But unless you can supply a perpetual grin to go with it, the comic mask is not as successful as other expressions in a half mask.

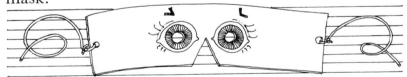

Surprise or fright: Draw two round, wide-open eyes, and place heavy eyebrows far above them. The higher the eyebrows, the stronger the emotion. Try making eyebrows with half-circles and with upside-down V's and decide which works better.

Anger: This is one of the easiest expressions to show. Both the eyes and the eyebrows slant down toward the nose. The more they slant, the fiercer they look.

Good humor: Draw oval eyes tapered up slightly at the outer corners and upward-curving eyelashes. Curving lines produce a pleasant expression.

Clowns: Characteristic vertical lines drawn above and below the eyes and horizontal lines extended out from the corners make a clown face when you add

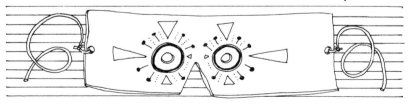

them to a sad, happy, or surprised expression.

Remember that a good mask exaggerates an already exaggerated expression. Furthermore, it is a fixed expression. A person's face is constantly changing, but a mask is always the same.

Eye masks are subtle and need some costuming to heighten the illusion and complete the effect. A head scarf tied under the chin creates a peasant woman character with an angry, surprised, sad-eyed, or even flirtatious look. A cloth cap creates a peasant man. The scarf tied low on the forehead with the knot in the back suggests a fiendish pirate. A silly hat or a snug knitted cap is appropriate for a clown.

How to make animal masks:

You can create certain bird and animal masks by adding beaks, ears, horns, manes, and whiskers. Here are some suggestions:

Cat Mask

1. Cut a pattern 6 inches by 11 inches and fold it in half crosswise. Measure 3½ inches along the fold

from the bottom edge and make a mark. Then measure 1½ inches along the bottom edge from the fold and make another mark. Draw a line to join these two points, and cut along the line through the folded paper. This makes room for your nose and mouth. To locate the eyes, measure 1¼ inches from the fold on each side, even with the top of the nose cutout. Cut out ½-inch circles as described on page 12. Transfer the pattern to black paper or cardboard.

2. For a pet pussycat or wild jungle beast, start with the eyes, bright yellow ovals that turn up slightly and have vertical green pupils.

3. Cut the lower part of the mask in a spreading fan of whiskers with spaces between. Or paint or draw on whiskers, or glue on strips of white paper or pipe cleaners.

4. Glue or tape triangular pointed ears to the top of the mask, above the eyes.

Owl Mask

1. Cut a mask 3½ inches by 11 inches. When you

cut out the triangle for the nose, leave it attached at the narrow end as a flap for a beak.

2. Draw or paint the eyes as a series of circles, one inside the other. Start with the pupil and work out. The center of each larger circle is always a bit farther away from the beak; the circles almost touch each other near the beak.

3. To give the impression of a beak, draw a large upside-down triangle on the mask between the glaring eyes. The broad part of the triangle, above the eyes, should be about 5 inches wide. The sides of the triangle curve inward around the eyes, and the sharp point of the triangle extends down to the bottom of the nose flap. A narrow, sharp triangle, perhaps only 2 inches wide at the top, is much fiercer-looking— more like a hawk or an eagle. Crease the flap down the middle to make it fit better over your own "beak."

4. For a crest, glue or tape one or more strips of fringed paper at the top of the mask. To make the fringe, cut a 2-inch-wide strip of construction paper;

draw a line ½ inch from one long edge and cut narrow strips as far as the line. Glue the fringed paper along the top of the mask so that it stands up like a crest. For a thicker fringe, cut another strip 2½ inches wide. Curl the fringe around a pencil if you like.

Mask with Horns and Ears

Some animals are more easily characterized by their horns or ears than by their eyes. Although you can make your animal masks all in one piece, it is usually easier, especially in the experimental stage, to make ears and horns separately and to glue, staple, or tape them in place.

Cow: Make half-circle ears and horns that are shaped like quarter-moons. Set them above good-humored brown eyes with long lashes, painted on or cut from fringe.

Bull: Make the ears pointed, the horns larger than the cow's, and the eyes angry.

Rabbit: Cut tall, stand-up ears from lightweight cardboard. Add whiskers and mildly surprised eyes.

Dog: For a beagle or spaniel, make sad eyes and flop-down ears cut from lightweight paper—a paper bag, for example.

Horse: Make short stand-up ears from lightweight cardboard with a mane of fringed paper, yarn, or string drooping down between them.

How to make a fantasy mask:

Some of the greatest fun of mask making comes from letting your imagination run free and creating designs that are not necessarily supposed to look like anything in particular. Paper masks are especially good for this kind of freewheeling project because they can be made quickly with inexpensive materials. If the first one doesn't turn out the way you want it, you can throw it away and make another.

Domino Mask and Hood

The domino mask, a plain black mask popular with actors in the past, is one extreme of the fantasy mask. It is blank and featureless, meant to conceal the eyes and to convey a sense of mystery and intrigue. The Lone Ranger wore a domino mask, and so did

Harlequin in the *commedia dell'arte*. Many of the merrymakers at masquerade balls felt freer to have fun when they could conceal their real identities behind a simple domino.

The domino is the basic half mask shaped like a pair of goggles. Black is traditional, but you can make it any color you like.

At one time the domino was always worn with a hood to cover the hair.

To make a hood, choose a piece of plain fabric in black or white, unless you are costuming a specific character like Little Red Riding Hood. Cut it 12 inches by 30 inches. Fold it in half crosswise, with the right side on the inside, so that the folded piece measures 12 inches by 15 inches. Pin the two layers along one 15-inch edge. Measure and mark ½ inch from that edge for a seamline. Sew the seam by machine or by hand with small running stitches, stopping ½ inch in from the raw edge.

To hem the remaining edges, turn ½ inch of each cut edge toward the wrong side and crease it. Then fold the cut edge in toward the crease. Pin the hem.

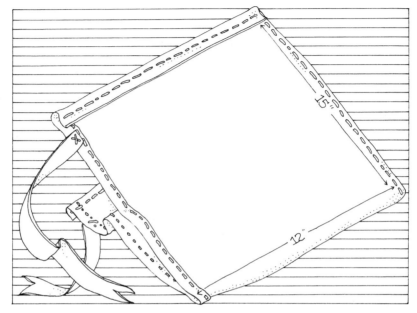

Sew by machine or by hand with hemming stitches. Turn right side out. Pin the hood under the chin, or sew on two ribbons for tying.

Painted Masks

At the opposite extreme from the plain domino is a half mask that has been decorated with paints and crayons in a variety of fantastic designs. For example, in place of the eyes, paint big flowers with the pupil at the center and bright petals blooming around it. Or draw two big twinkling stars. Or design a geometric pattern of circles, lines, and squares, or a freeform arrangement of dots and swirls.

Decorated Masks

A paper half mask can form the base of an interesting miniature sculpture. Attach feathers to it, or dangle beads and tiny bells from it. Glue to it bits of leather or metal or pieces of fabric or fake fur. Make sure, however, that the decorations are not too heavy for the stiff paper and that there are no sharp edges that could injure you when you put the mask on.

Headdresses

Even the simplest mask becomes dramatic and important-looking with the addition of a headdress. You can make one by extending the top of the basic half mask, making it at least 6 inches high instead of 3½ inches, so that it covers the forehead and hair. The simplest variation is the crown, made by cutting the top in a saw-tooth pattern and then painting and decorating it as royally as you wish.

Or cut and paint it to resemble a wreath of flowers or stars or hearts.

Let the materials you have on hand be the inspiration for the design. The best directions for making a fantasy headdress come from inside your own head.

CHAPTER 3

Spirit Masks of Fall:
Helmet and Stick Masks

Like many of our holidays and festivals, Halloween is a combination of customs—ancient and new, pagan and religious, frightening and fun. Its origins go back perhaps two thousand years, to the Celts of what is now called Ireland and Scotland. They observed the beginning of the new year on November 1, a day that was also the festival of the dead.

On the night before, the souls of the dead were thought to be flying around—not only the kindly souls of departed relatives and friends, but also witches and goblins and other evil spirits that could certainly make trouble. The custom of building huge bonfires on October 31 was partly to celebrate the beginning of a new year with new fire; it was also a way to frighten away the scary spirits.

Then in the seventh century, Pope Boniface IV decided that a special day in honor of the church's saints and martyrs should fall on November 1, the same day as this pagan festival. As people were gradually converted to Christianity, they clung to some of their old beliefs and their old celebrations: They still believed that ghosts flew on the night before All Saints' Day (or All Hallows, as it was called then), but Halloween (All Hallows' Eve) became a time of merrymaking, often with masks to disguise the identity of the revelers and also to frighten off any evil spirits that might be lurking about.

Although our custom of Halloween has been derived from the ancient Celts in particular, it seems

that many people all over the world have shared the same mixed feelings about the dead—reverence and veneration for one's ancestors, together with the uneasy feeling that spirits might inhabit the body of an enemy and be anything but friendly.

Among such people, the mask has always been extremely important. Eskimos, American Indians, African tribes—all have used elaborate masks to impersonate or to relate to the spirits of the dead.

For this reason, the mask maker was a person of high status in his tribe or village and was the only person allowed to make the elaborate masks worn in sacred rituals. He often inherited his position, but in some societies he was chosen for his talent while still very young from a select group among the tribe. In either case, his training lasted for many years, frequently in secret. He was often exempted from dangerous and time-consuming activities, such as fighting and hunting, in order to create the masks that were vital to the spiritual well-being of his community.

There was a time when only certain people were allowed to wear masks. In primitive societies, masks were generally used only by men, and in some cultures a woman was put to death if she even looked at one of the sacred masks. In other cultures, however, women also had secret societies, and their leaders wore masks in some of the rites.

Mask makers created different kinds of masks for many different purposes, and they used whatever materials were available in their part of the world; the variety is seemingly endless. Some masks had to be precise in the execution of symbolism; others allowed greater freedom in the mask maker's interpretation. Styles varied, too. Some were made to be held on sticks in front of the wearer's face, or the wearer bit on a stick or strap or little knob built into the back of the mask. Later, masks tied behind the wearer's head. There was also the helmet, or *casque,* mask, which covered the entire head and rested on the shoulders. And of course there was the domino.

Like the primitive mask makers, you can create

masks from whatever you have on hand. A helmet mask can be made from a paper bag, construction paper, poster board, cardboard box, metal can, plastic jug, or straw basket. There are three requirements for such a helmet mask: It should fit comfortably without any sharp edges or dangerous projections, either inside or out; you should be able to breathe easily; and you should be able to see clearly where you're going. You will also need a variety of materials for decorating the mask.

Iroquois Mask

The Iroquois Indians, from the region east of the Great Lakes, continued to make masks long after most other American Indian tribes had abandoned the art. Their secret False Face Society was responsible for making masks to ward off the evil spirits, especially those that caused sickness. These masks were very frightening-looking, with human features that were grotesquely twisted and misshapen.

Spirit Masks of Fall: Helmet and Stick Masks

The mask maker carved the mask directly onto a living tree, usually a linden. First he chose an appropriate tree, prayed to its spirit, burned an offering of tobacco for it, and then began to carve. When he had finished, he cut the carved mask away from the tree—carefully, so as not to kill the tree—and painted it. Unless you are a skilled woodcarver, however, you will find it easier to reproduce this mask on an ordinary brown paper bag.

What you will need:

A brown paper bag, 5 inches by 8 inches or larger; pencil and scissors; tempera (poster) paints and paintbrushes.

How to construct the mask:

1. Turn up a wide cuff all around the open end of the paper bag so that when you put the bag over your head, the bottom of the bag rests firmly on the top of your head. Cut the cuff into strips about ¼ inch to ½ inch wide, to make a fringe. The fringe will hang over your shoulders.

2. Put the bag over your head with the seam in the back. With your fingers, locate the position of your eyes and nose. Mark them lightly with a pencil. Be very careful that the pencil does not pierce the paper, because if you press too hard you could injure your eyes. Take off the bag and cut out two eyeholes and a 2-inch flap for your nose. Leave the flap attached. Try on the bag again and make sure you can see and breathe.

How to decorate the mask:

Flatten the paper bag. Select three bright colors, such as red, white, and yellow. Paint the features with bold, sweeping strokes of color. The features should not match, and they should be lopsided. Begin with the eyes, making one larger than the other. Paint a crooked nose and make the mouth twist to one side, with perhaps one large tooth sticking out. Don't try to add small details.

Although this is designed to resemble an Iroquois False Face, you can vary the features to create almost any kind of face you want—a grinning orange jack-o'-lantern, for instance, or a somber death skull.

Kachina Mask

Not all masks were supposed to be frightening. In the American Southwest, the Pueblo Indians believed in dozens of friendly little gods called kachinas who had supposedly brought water and corn to their people. When the kachinas returned to the lake where they lived, they left behind masks so they could easily find their way back to the village to dance and have a good time. There are over a hundred of these goodhearted traditional gods, each honored with an appropriate mask and a special dance and ceremony performed by masked impersonators.

Kachina masks were of the helmet type, made of wood, leather, basketry, or gourds, decorated with fur and feathers and painted symbolically according to an exact formula. The men who made the kachina

masks took great care in the placement of each feather and each dab of paint; to do the job incorrectly might displease the otherwise kindly gods.

You can make bright, playful masks like kachina masks with construction paper. The mask you make may not cause rain to fall or corn to grow because you will be following your own ideas rather than ancient tradition, but who knows what might happen?

What you will need:

Construction paper in several bright colors; pencil and scissors; tape or glue.

How to construct the mask:

1. Tape or glue together two or more pieces of construction paper—turquoise, for instance—to make a cylinder that just fits over your head. The size of construction paper sometimes varies. If each sheet is 12 inches long, two sheets taped end to end may be enough; if the sheets are smaller, you can join the ends with strips of a contrasting color—orange, for instance—one on each side.

2. Try on the paper cylinder. With your fingers, locate the position of your eyes and mark them lightly with a pencil. Be sure never to pierce the paper, because if you do you might injure your eyes. Take off the cylinder and cut out two square eyeholes. Since the mask is open at the top and bottom, you can probably breathe freely; if not, cut another hole for your nose.

How to decorate the mask:

Think of the kachina mask as a paper sculpture, pleasing to look at rather than scary or horrible. Unlike the Iroquois masks with their dramatically exaggerated features, the kachina masks are rather restrained.

Kachina mask shapes are generally geometric rather than realistic. Balance is important, but the left and right sides of the face often do not match. The eyes, for instance, could be orange rectangles placed next to the eyeholes you have cut in the turquoise cylinder, one extending all the way to a yellow ear that sprouts like a wing from one side of the head. Instead of putting a matching ear on the opposite side, you might fashion a large horn that extends out or swoops upward.

Real kachina masks were often decorated with fur, feathers, and other natural materials. The idea of this paper-sculpture kachina is to *suggest* rather than to *look like*. For instance, a fur collar could be suggested by gluing on rows of paper fringe. Although you may further decorate the mask with poster paint or crayons, kachinas seem more effective if you stick with construction paper in bright colors and simple shapes.

Tuscarora Harvest Mask

One of the six nations of the Iroquois, the Tuscarora Indians of the Eastern United States honored the spirits of the autumn harvest with masks made of woven cornhusks. You can make a similar mask out of woven construction paper, held in front of the face on a stick.

What you will need:

Poster board; three sheets of construction paper: yellow, orange or tan, and brown or black; pencil, ruler, scissors, and glue; a flat stick, such as a paint paddle; masking tape.

How to make the mask:

1. Draw lines the length of the yellow and orange or tan construction paper ½ inch apart. Cut the yellow paper into strips to within ¾ inch of the end of the paper; leave the strips connected. Cut the orange or tan paper into separate ½-inch strips and weave them through the yellow. Round off the square corners and put a dot of glue between some of the strips to keep them from coming unwoven.

2. Cut wide triangles from brown or black paper to

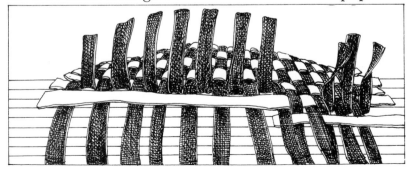

make eyes and a mouth. Glue them in place on the woven background.

3. Cut a 9-inch circle of poster board. Make a handle from a flat stick, or glue together two pieces of poster board, 12 inches by 3 inches. Attach the handle to the center of the circle with masking tape or glue. Glue the woven mask to the other side of the circle.

Eskimo Spirit Masks

The Eskimos believed in animal spirits. Like many Indian tribes, the Eskimos felt a kinship with animals, birds, and fish that they thought could assume human form. They believed that one of these creatures may have been the founder, or the ancestor, of a family or clan; they showed special consideration to that animal ancestor, which was called a totem. Some Indian tribes carved and painted totem poles in honor of their animal ancestor. Other peoples, like the Eskimos, made totem masks, some of which were worn by a shaman, or medicine man, as he practiced his art.

Spirit Masks of Fall: Helmet and Stick Masks

What you will need:

A sturdy white paper plate or poster board; scissors and pencil; a flat stick, such as a paint paddle; masking tape; glue; typing paper; clear tape; staples; construction paper; crayons or tempera (poster) paints and paintbrushes; odds and ends for decoration; yarn or string.

How to construct the basic mask:

1. Cut a 10-inch circle of poster board or use a paper plate. Make a handle from a flat stick or glue together two pieces of poster board 12 inches by 3 inches. Attach the handle to the circle with masking tape or glue.

2. Cut four pieces of typing paper ($8\frac{1}{2}$ by 11 inches) in half diagonally. Starting at the square corner, roll toward the diagonal edge, keeping the tube tight and even like a large drinking straw. Tape it with clear tape to keep it from unrolling. Make seven tubes. Or cut seven strips of poster board, $\frac{1}{2}$ inch wide and about 12 inches long. Arrange the tubes or

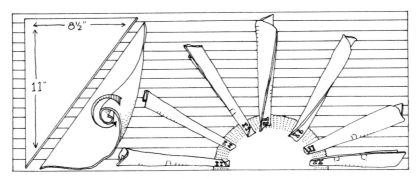

strips around the circle, like rays of the sun, overlapping the edge of the circle by at least 2 inches,
so that they stand out without drooping. Fasten them
with staples or masking tape.

How to decorate the mask:

Making the basic stick mask is easy; even decorating
it is no problem once you know how you want it to
look. But deciding on its appearance can take a
great deal of thought. First you must choose your
totem—your spiritual ancestor. Then you must
think of ways to symbolize your totem. Here are a
few suggestions:

Flower totem: Paint a sunflower face, not necessarily

a realistic one, on a paper plate. Then use construction paper to make seven small flowers, simple ones cut from one piece of paper or more elaborate ones with separate petals. Make them all alike or in different sizes and colors. Glue or staple them to one end of each of the seven strips.

Bird totem: Paint a fierce bird beak on the mask, or glue a folded paper beak to the front of it. Tie bunches of real bluejay or other bird feathers to the strips with yarn. Or cut out bird shapes or wing shapes from construction paper and glue or staple them to the ends of the strips.

Fish totem: Cut fish shapes from construction paper and attach them to the strips with short pieces of yarn or string so that the fish will move, giving the impression that they have been "hooked."

Animal totem: Draw pictures of an animal that you think would be an appropriate totem for you, or cut out a colored picture from a magazine and glue the picture on the front of the mask. Tie bits of fur or other small objects on the ends of the strips.

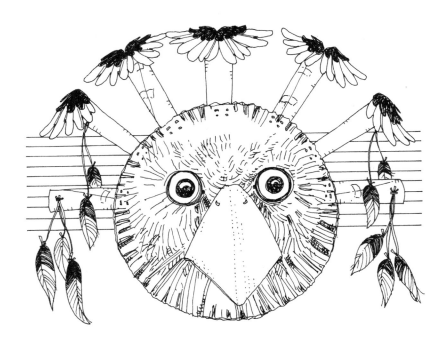

None of these masks is a Halloween mask in the familiar sense. But all of them are drawn from ancient traditions that mixed fear, reverence, and acceptance of the spirits that were believed to inhabit the earth.

CHAPTER 4

Carnival Masks of Winter:
Head Masks

The sun, the source of light and warmth and perhaps the most powerful and changeable element in the lives of primitive people, was worshiped with awe and watched with dread as the days grew shorter and colder. But when the winter solstice arrived, marking the shortest day in the year and the point at which the days began gradually to lengthen, it was a time to celebrate. Perhaps because people needed cheering up during the long nights, winter became a season for merrymaking (and sometimes mischief-making, too).

Citizens of ancient Rome who were followers of a pagan sun god called Mithras celebrated the winter solstice, which fell on December 25 in the old calendar, as the birthday of the Unconquered Sun. At about the same time, other Romans used the festival of Saturn, the god of agriculture, as an excuse for wild parties called Saturnalia. Fourth-century Christians decided this was an appropriate time to observe the anniversary of the birth of Christ, whom they called "the light of the world." The reasoning of the Church fathers was practical: Christianity was opposed by the Roman rulers, but with so much revelry going on at one time, the persecutors would be unlikely to take notice of any religious celebration by a small band of Christians. And the Christians, most of them converts from pagan religions, were happy to have their own festivities to participate in at that time of year.

Through the years, people found additional reasons for winter merrymaking. Carnivals, during which the entire community took part in religious celebrations, usually had their roots in ancient observances of the coming of spring and new life, and involved a great deal of folklore and superstition that had little to do with the religious occasion. Adopting an attitude of "If you can't fight them, join them," the Church gave up trying to eliminate the old non-Christian traditions and simply made them part of the Christian holiday.

In Bavaria, Germany, the carnival season called *Fasching* began on January 6—the Epiphany, or the feast of the Wise Men. But in other Roman Catholic countries, the carnival of Mardi Gras—literally meaning "fat Tuesday"—was a last chance to eat, drink, and be merry before Lent, a somber period of fasting and penance, which began the next day, Ash Wednesday. Mardi Gras celebrations have been popular for many years in New Orleans and Rio de Janeiro, as well as in major cities and tiny hamlets throughout Europe and South America.

Masks are an important part of the winter carnival season, a time when everyone seems to like to try out a new identity and pretend to be someone he or she is not. In the masked balls of the Middle Ages, wealthy noblemen disguised themselves as peasants, freeing themselves for a while from the restrictions placed on them by their wealth and rank. At the same time, peasants masqueraded as nobility; although no better fed or housed than usual, they were allowed the privilege of speaking and acting as though they had high social status.

In some carnival parades, the masks are actually gigantic heads, intricately constructed and elaborately painted. They are placed on top of the head, and the wearer must peer out through some other part of the costume. You can make an oversize head quite simply by using a grocery bag as a base on which to build a papier-mâché shell.

Papier-Mâché Head Masks

All kinds of masks, from the precisely realistic to the

wildly improbable, can be made with papier-mâché. Pronounced PAY–per ma–SHAY in English and meaning "chewed paper" in French (although it probably originated in China), papier-mâché is a material that has been used by craftsmen for about two thousand years. It is made by tearing paper, dipping the pieces in paste, and then building them up, layer by layer, over a mold. When the paper layers dry, they form a rigid, lightweight shell that is comfortable to wear and easy to decorate.

What you will need:

For the basic mask: A large grocery bag; a pile of newspapers; masking tape; a cookie sheet; flour, water, a bowl or shallow pan, and a fork; several lightweight paper bags; tempera (poster) paints or latex wall paint and paintbrushes; a large-eyed needle and strong thread, such as fishing line or dental floss; fabric, pen or chalk.

For elaborate masks: Construction paper, pencil, and ruler; sequins, glitter, metallic paint; paper cups, plastic margarine containers, cardboard tubes, jar lids, poster board, and other odds and ends for building facial features.

How to make the mold:

1. Stuff a large grocery bag with crumpled newspaper to within 3 inches of the top of the bag. Stuff the bag so that it is fairly firm but not rock-hard. Fold the remaining 3 inches of the bag toward the center, making small pleats around the opening, and fasten down with a couple of strips of masking tape

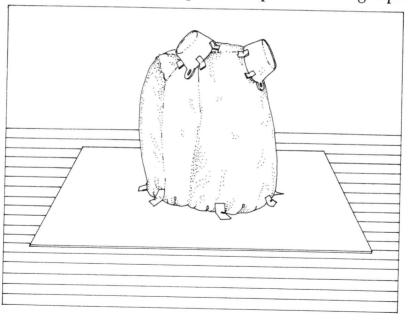

—this is the collar. Turn over the stuffed bag and tape it, open end down, to a cookie sheet.

2. Press and mold the stuffed bag until it is an oval head shape, rounding off the corners and taping them to hold the shape. You can leave the head plain, or build up features, such as a nose and ears, with cups, lids, and other odds and ends, taping them in place.

How to construct the mask:

1. Lay several sheets of newspaper together, and tear them into strips 2 or 3 inches wide and about 1 foot long. Do not cut the strips; tearing feathers the edges so that no ridges will show where the strips overlap and the surface will be smooth.

2. Put 1 cup of flour in a bowl or pan; slowly stir in 2 cups of cold water with a fork to make a smooth, creamy paste. Protect your work area with sheets of newspaper—this is a messy business.

3. Dip each strip of paper into the paste and wipe off the excess with your thumb and finger. If you have added features to the head, cover them first

with slightly overlapping strips. Then begin at the bottom of the head and work up to the top, covering it completely with a layer of strips that go around the head and ending with strips that go across the top.

4. Tear the lightweight paper bags into strips, dip them in the paste, and cover the head completely with a layer of strips that go in the opposite direction from the first layer—up and down, instead of around. As you go along, keep smoothing the strips with your fingers, working in the paste, to make sure the surface of the mask is as even as possible.

5. Add two more layers, one of newspapers and one of brown paper, always applying the strips in the opposite direction from the layer beneath. Let the head dry for a couple of days.

How to decorate the mask:

1. Leave the mask, with the stuffing still inside, on the cookie sheet to make it easier to work on. Give the mask two coats of paint in the base color. "White" skin color is made by adding a little red and a dash of brown to white paint. For dark skin, start with brown paint; lighten the brown with white or darken it with black. Then decorate the mask to look like the carnival figure you have chosen. Begin with the eyes; the usual rule is to place the eyes about halfway between the top of the head and the chin. The distance between the eyes is about the same as the width of one eye. Once you have located them, the other features are not difficult. When the paint is dry, add hair or other details, according to the character.

2. Remove the head from the cookie sheet, pull off

the tape, and gently remove the newspaper stuffing. Thread a needle and make large (1-inch) running stitches around the collar 1 inch from the edge of the opening of the bag. Leave both ends of thread long so you can adjust the size of the opening to your head. Allow this unstiffened and unpainted collar to fold back toward the inside of the mask.

3. The mask should not come down over your head like a helmet; it should sit on top of your head, supported by the collar and wedged down over your forehead (but not over your eyes) to hold it in place. Draw the thread just tight enough so that the opening in the collar is big enough for the top of your head, but not so big that the mask will suddenly slip down. Wearing a knitted cap under it will also help to keep it in place. For added stability, stuff the head lightly with crumpled newspaper.

4. A piece of plain fabric draped over your own head will conceal your face and blend into the rest of the costume. You can use a discarded sheer silk scarf or cut a 24-inch square from an old sheet or pillowcase or some other lightweight fabric. Ar-

range the square over your head with one of the corners hanging down in front so that your face is completely hidden. Cover your eye with one hand (under the fabric) and with the other hand mark the fabric with pen or chalk where the eyehole should be. Then do the other eye. Remove the fabric from your head and cut out holes that are large enough for you to see clearly. Never cut the fabric when you are wearing it. If the fabric is sheer, you might not need a breathing hole, but if the fabric is heavy, it is wise to cut another hole near your nose and mouth. Line up the holes so that you can see and breathe easily, add the knitted cap if you need it for a good fit, and put on the mask, adjusting it so that it rests firmly on your head. Wrap another scarf or a length of the same fabric around your neck to help blend the cloth covering your face into the rest of the costume.

Sun God and Snowman Masks

Everyone is always glad to see the return of the sun,

with lengthening hours of daylight and increasing warmth.

1. To make a sun god mask, begin with a plain head mask. Paint it bright yellow or gold.

2. Cut out a dozen pairs of triangles 7 inches tall and 3 inches wide at the base, from orange and yellow construction paper. Draw a line ½ inch from each base and bend along the line. Glue each pair of triangles together at the apex (the top), the bases bent in toward each other. Arrange the pairs of triangles around the top and sides of the head to re-

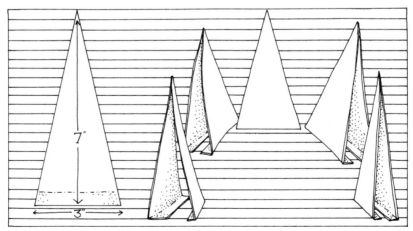

semble rays. Overlap the bases so that each pair of triangles is slightly in front of or behind the one next to it. You can vary the height of the triangles to make the head seem rounder. Glue each pair of triangles on the head and spread the bases of each pair two inches apart so the rays don't droop.

3. Paint red or orange features on the mask to make a face.

4. Drape your head with yellow fabric (see p. 57, #4). Wear the mask with a bright yellow or orange shirt, or drape yourself in a yellow blanket or bedspread.

Make a snowman, the typical figure of winter, from a plain head mask painted white and decorated with black features. To make a carrot nose, roll a 9-inch by 12-inch sheet of orange construction paper into a long, thin cone; attach it by making a series of ½-inch cuts around the wide end of the cone, bending out the tabs that are formed, and gluing them in place. A white cloth over your face (see p. 57, #4), a bright-colored knitted scarf, and a white sheet complete the costume.

Janus, the Two-faced God

Janus, one of the principal Roman deities, was the guardian of gates and doors and the god of beginnings. His festival was celebrated on the first day of the new year. January takes its name from Janus, who was usually portrayed with two bearded faces placed back to back so that he could look in two directions at the same time.

1. Make a plain head mask and add a nose on both front and back. To make a simple nose, cut a 3-inch by 5-inch rectangle from stiff paper. Measure 1½ inches from each end on one long side, and draw lines from there to the corner on the other long side. Fold up the two triangular flaps to form a shape 2 inches wide at the top and 5 inches wide at the bottom. Bend the shape to form a nose, and glue the flaps to the face after you've located the eyes and know where the nose should go. Make a second nose for the back. Paint over the noses when you paint the head.

2. Paint faces front and back. Paint on dark brown

hair and a beard that joins at the sideburns. Glue rows of fringed paper over the painted hair and beard. To make the fringe, cut 3-inch-wide strips of brown construction paper; draw a line ½ inch from one long edge and cut narrow strips as far as the line. Curl the fringe around a pencil if you like.

3. Add a white cloth over your face (see p. 57, #4), and dress in a sheet draped like a Roman toga.

Mardi Gras King and Queen

These are good masks on which to try out some fantasy decoration. Mardi Gras masks are noted for their extravagant ornamentation. Start by giving them outlandish makeup—sweeping eyelashes cut from construction paper, silvered eyelids, glitter-dusted cheeks, sequin beauty marks and freckles. Make hair of satiny ribbon formed in loops and glued on in rows. You might even want to make black dominos, so that your king and queen can be masked, too.

Make crowns of poster board strips 6 inches high and long enough to go around the head. Cut in a saw-tooth pattern and decorate with fake jewels.

Over your face wear a blue or purple cloth (see p. 57, #4) decorated with shiny stars, and dress in a long, regal cape.

Dragons and Other Terrific Monsters

The Chinese New Year falls sometime between mid-January and mid-February and is an occasion for feasting, setting off firecrackers, and staging gala parades. To the Chinese the dragon, a mythical beast usually shown as a winged, fire-breathing reptile, is a symbol of fertility and prosperity. Representations of the dragon are usually featured in the Chinese New Year parade.

1. Use a bag head as a base for a dragon mask. The dragon, like any monster, needs bulging eyes. Tape on small paper cups. Add a paper or plastic container for a snout; cover the plastic with at least one layer of papier-mâché.

2. Paint the dragon bright green with red eyes and nostrils and with a fierce white fanged mouth outlined in black. Cut a long, forked tongue from red construction paper and glue it between the bared white fangs so it hangs out of the fire-breathing mouth.

3. Cover your face with green fabric (see p. 57, #4) beneath the dragon's head, and dress in something green. Two people under a green bedspread, one of them wearing the dragon head, make a fine monster for a New Year's parade.

The dragon is just one kind of imaginary monster. Since everyone loves frightening monsters, and since everyone has his own ideas of what a monster ought to look like, you can invent one all your own. Add all kinds of grotesque features—horns, popping-out eyes, antennae, and so on—using odds and ends like small boxes and bottle caps. Paint your mask in weird colors and have a monstrous time.

CHAPTER 5

Portrait Masks of Spring:
Face Masks

As we've already discussed, the earliest masks were made for religious purposes, to help people deal with a universe that was a mystery to them, a universe in which the supernatural and the natural were equally real. Later, when religious ritual evolved into drama, masks changed in form and function. Today, masks are seldom used in the theater, and the purpose of the mask has changed as well.

Some masks are used strictly for fun. Others have purely practical purposes—masks that protect their wearers from germs and fumes and welding sparks, from hockey sticks and fencing foils. There are masks that allow a person to breathe under water or on the surface of the moon. And of course masks are sometimes used by criminals to make a getaway without being identified.

At times in recent history, life masks were made directly on the human face in order to preserve an exact likeness of that person. Many famous men suffered through the ordeal of having a plaster of Paris cast applied to their faces and sitting immobilized and miserable until the plaster set. Not only was the process uncomfortable, it was also dangerous. Thomas Jefferson reportedly nearly suffocated when his life mask was attempted. A less troublesome approach was the death mask, made just after the subject's demise. One obvious drawback, of course, was that the subject was not around to admire the results.

Another approach was to duplicate a particular face as realistically as possible by making a mask on a sculptured mold. The Polish-American artist Wladyslaw Benda made the "social mask" fashionable in the 1920s when celebrities crowded his studio to have him reproduce their likeness in mask form. While these realistic masks were popular for a time, they never really succeeded as an art form, seeming static and lifeless in comparison to a piece of fine sculpture. Still, Benda, who died in 1948, was regarded as an expert in the craft of realistic mask making.

Papier-Mâché Face Masks

You can make portrait masks with features that are as realistic or as exaggerated as you wish by building a papier-mâché shell on a sculptured mold. The mold will determine how the finished mask will look; the base for the mold allows the mask to curve around your face, completely covering it but giving you room to breathe. Forming the entire mold from clay would require several pounds of it; instead, use a mixing bowl for a base and model the features on it in clay, creating nose, chin, eyebrows, and cheekbones as a sculptor would. The results may be grotesquely ugly or sweetly pretty, but they will have the form of a real face.

What you will need:

For the mold: 2 pounds of plasticine modeling clay, wax paper, a 2½-quart mixing bowl, plastic wrap, and ruler.

For the papier-mâché: Newspapers, flour, water, a bowl or shallow pan, a fork.

For decorating and finishing: Tempera (poster) paints and paintbrushes, scissors, sharp-pointed knife, string, large-eyed needle and thread, yarn, and other decorative materials.

How to make the mold:

1. Knead about one pound of plasticine bit by bit with your hands until it is soft and workable. Press it into a flat circle or oval between pieces of wax paper, using your hands or a rolling pin. Peel off the

paper and flip the circle of clay onto the bowl. It should just cover the bowl.

2. Locate the position of the features on the clay circle, sketching them in with your fingernail or a small knife. The general rule is to place the eyes halfway between the top of the head and the chin; the tip of the nose halfway between the eyes and the chin; and the mouth one-third of the way between the tip of the nose and the chin. Make the centers of the eyes exactly 2½ inches apart. The space between the eyes is usually the same as the width of the nose and about the same as the width of one eye.

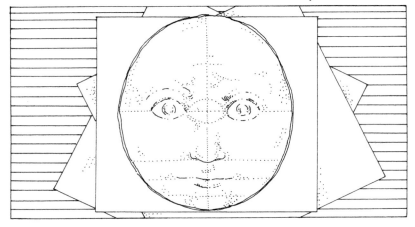

3. Soften the rest of the clay and begin building up the features of the face. When you put the papier-mâché over the model, you will lose a lot of detail, so all the features should be exaggerated. Make deep eye sockets, bulging eyes, thick eyebrows, a big nose, pronounced cheekbones, a jutting chin. Keep the curves smoothly rounded, and avoid undercuts—if you make the nose hook too much, for example,

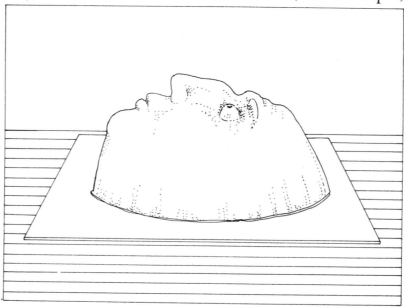

you will have a hard time removing the mask from the mold.

4. Cover the clay mold completely with a sheet of plastic wrap, taking care that it clings to the details as much as possible. This will allow you to remove the mask easily from the clay.

How to construct the mask:

1. Lay several sheets of newspaper together and tear them into strips about 1 inch wide and 1 foot long. Don't cut the strips; tearing feathers the edges so that no ridges will show where they overlap, and the surface will be smoother.

2. Put ½ cup of flour in a shallow pan and slowly stir in 1 cup of cold water with a fork to make a smooth, creamy paste. Protect your work area with newspaper.

3. Dip each strip of paper into the paste and wipe off the excess between your thumb and finger. Beginning with the nose, completely cover the mold with overlapping strips, all running out from the center,

like spokes in a wheel. For some areas, you will need to tear the strips into smaller pieces.

4. Beginning again with the nose, lay a second layer of strips across the first layer so that they run in the opposite direction, going around and around like a pinwheel, ending with strips that circle the outside edge. This will not work perfectly on certain areas, such as the eyes, but it will be easier around the chin, cheeks, and forehead. Add two more layers, the third in the same direction as the first, and the fourth like the second, working and smoothing the strips with your fingers to make the surface of the mask as even as possible.

5. Allow the mask to dry completely—at least overnight and possibly a few days in damp weather. It may warp out of shape if it is still damp. Work it carefully off the mold, pulling gently on the edges of the plastic wrap to help release it. Trim the edges with scissors. You may need to cut away some of the mask under the chin for a better fit. The mold may be used again as it is, or you can alter it as you wish.

How to finish and decorate the mask:

1. Reinforce the inside edge of the mask with a strip of masking tape or with additional strips of papier-mâché.

2. Cut out openings for the eyes, nostrils, and mouth with a small sharp knife. Try on the mask. Make sure you can see clearly and breathe freely—this mask can get very hot and stuffy if the holes are too small. Enlarge the holes if necessary.

3. Paint the mask with one or two coats of paint in the base color. You can paint the inside, too, but it's not necessary. Then paint the features according to the character you are creating.

4. Hold the mask in place with one hand, and with a pencil in the other hand mark a spot near the reinforced edge just above each ear. Remove the mask, punch small holes, and tie a piece of string through each hole. Tie the strings behind your head. If the mask sags, punch another hole at the top and add another string that goes back over your head and ties onto the other strings. If the mask is too large

and the eyeholes seem too low, insert padding, such as a wad of paper, inside the top where the mask rests on your head.

May Bride and Bridegroom Masks

After a dark, cold winter that may have exhausted food supplies, the arrival of spring was greeted with enthusiastic celebration in many European countries of long ago. Even after people became more sophisticated about their natural world, they celebrated the end of winter by "driving out" witches and demons in order to welcome the coming of the planting season, represented by attractive figures like the pretty May bride.

The first day of May was originally celebrated as a spring festival in honor of the goddesses of fertility. Much later, the occasion was observed with pretty young girls decked out as brides. Since brides everywhere in the world are invariably beautiful, the mask must be a beautiful one. The mask of the May bride can be adapted for practically any fair damsel you

can think of—Snow White, Gretel, Cinderella, dainty princess, or robust country maiden, a blue-eyed blonde or a brown-eyed brunette.

How to make the mask:

1. Model her features carefully. You will still have to exaggerate them in order not to lose the details in the mask, but don't make them grotesque.

2. If she's a Nordic type, paint on a creamy complexion: white, with a few drops of red and a dash of brown. Give her clear white eyes with sweet blue irises, long dark lashes, innocently arched eyebrows, rosy pink cheeks (by adding more red to the pale flesh color), and a heart-shaped red mouth. For a dark-skinned beauty, use brown paint toned lighter with white or deepened with black.

3. Make three bundles of yellow yarn, twenty strands each, a yard long. Tie each bundle in the center. With needle and thread, stitch the three bundles to the top of the mask; the stitches will form a "part" in her hair. Measure 8 inches on each side of

the part and stitch the bundles in place. Braid the bundles below the second set of stitches and tie bright ribbons at the end of each braid.

To make a fitting bridegroom for the May bride, a Hansel to accompany Gretel, or a Prince Charming to rescue any fair lady, make the cheekbones and jawbone squarer and more rugged on the sculptured mold. Darken the "white" complexion, and make the eyebrows and the mouth straight and serious. Paint on some hair, and consider making a yarn beard with a mustache stitched between the nose and upper lip.

Witch and Demon Masks

People have always been bothered by the problem of evil in the world. At one time people believed they could get rid of evil by driving out witches and demons on certain nights of the year when these creatures were roaming about freely. In some parts of the world, witches were associated with late fall and Halloween. But in other places a favorite time for witchery was the night before the first of May, called Walpurgis Night.

How to make the mask:

1. Form heavy cheekbones with hollow cheeks and sunken eyes. Make a large nose and pointy chin, but don't hook them or the mask will not come off the mold. Make heavy eyebrows, either arched high or pulled down in a frown. Once you have applied the layers of papier-mâché, add warts and other strange features with lumps of facial tissue soaked in the paste.

2. Paint the witch's face white or mix in a little green and black for added ghastliness. Give her huge white open eyes with black centers, bloodshot with streaks of red and bluish-purple bags that every self-respecting witch has under her eyes. Black out a couple of teeth in her nasty grin.

3. For the witch's straggly hair, use black yarn or grayish string. Make a 3-foot bundle of about 40 strands and tie it in the middle. Punch two small

holes in the reinforced edge at the top of the mask and tie the center of the bundle in place. Cut some of it in shaggy bangs. Tack the rest here and there with needle and black thread.

You can use the witch mold to make a demon mask. Change the expression slightly by remodeling the eyebrows. Remember that the angle of the eyebrows makes a great difference in a mask; those that slant down toward the nose always make a mask look sinister. Then paint the mask a different color— red darkened with black, or greenish yellow. Don't put long hair on the demon, but paint a black hairline that comes down to a point over his forehead, and give him sideburns, a small beard, and a thin mustache. Paint pointed ears on each side of his head.

Character Masks

As you become more expert at sculpturing the mold and painting the finished mask, a whole range of possibilities will open up. Although portrait masks demand more time and effort and skill than other types of masks, they offer great rewards. As you progress, you may want to explore new techniques in making these masks.

Although the mixing bowl is a convenient and economical base, its perfect roundness is a disadvantage. The human head is egg-shaped, and as you develop as a mask maker, you may want to try to duplicate that shape using a smaller base—a brick, for example, or a small box—building most or all of the mold from modeling clay.

Once the shape on which you are working becomes more realistic, you'll find ways to change the character in subtle ways: a stern face with a long, narrow nose and a thin, straight mouth; a jolly face with fat, bulging cheeks and crinkled-up eyes.

You'll learn tricks in painting, too—such as aging a character by adding lines across the forehead, around the eyes, and bracketing the nose and mouth. As you study faces and practice techniques, you'll learn to make faces that resemble the people you know.

Quick Papier-Mâché Masks

On the other hand, you may prefer face masks that can be made quickly, with no attempt at realism. In that case, the simple face mask offers unlimited opportunities for decoration.

What you will need:

A 2½-quart mixing bowl; cardboard scraps, tape, and plastic wrap; newspaper; materials for making and decorating the papier-mâché mask (see page 72).

How to make the mask:

1. To make three-dimensional features, tape cardboard scraps on the bowl as eyes, nose, and mouth. Keep the shapes strong and simple. Cover it with a sheet of plastic wrap.
2. Cut four sheets of newspaper a little larger than

the bowl. Spread other newspapers on your work surface.

3. Put ½ cup of flour in a small bowl and slowly stir in 1 cup of cold water with a fork to make a smooth, creamy paste.

4. Lay a sheet of cut newspaper on the protected work surface and spread some paste on it with your hand. Smear it generously over the paper, turn the paper over, and coat the other side. Lay the paste-coated paper over the bowl and press it gently with your hands until it fits the curve of the bowl and the contours of the features.

5. Repeat with each of the three remaining sheets of newspaper. Allow the mask to dry completely. Remove it from the mold and trim the edges with scissors. Then see "How to Finish and Decorate the Mask" on pages 77–78.

When you pick up your paintbrush, you can transform this plain face mask into anything at all —animal, human, superhuman—from any period in history or even beyond all time.

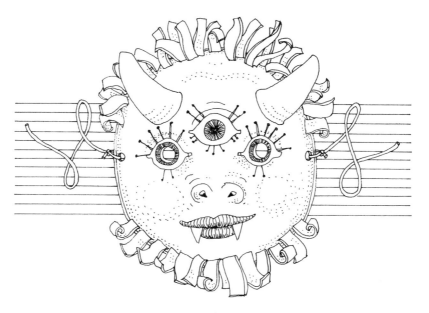

Whether you have tried all the kinds of masks in this book or sampled only a few, you have become, if only for a short time, a mask maker and mask wearer. You, like many others from the beginning of man's history, have shared the experience of creating a new image and of changing your identity for a little while. You, too, have been touched by mask magic, and *you* have made it happen.

Index